THE SAINTS WHO STRUGGLED WITH ADDICTION

PEOPLE ARE NOT DEFINED BY THEIR STRUGGLES AND FAILURES

HENRY SSERIISO

CONTENTS

INTRODUCTION

The night is far gone; the day is at hand. So then, let us cast off the works of darkness and put on the armor of light.

— ROMANS 13:12

No one wants to be addicted; this is the truth, no matter how the addiction started or how long it has been going on. It is hard to express to your family, friends, and loved ones exactly why it is so hard to beat addiction. You know that you want to change your life and overcome your addiction, but this is easier said than done.

However, there is no need to despair. Even when it seems like no treatment will work for you, there is always hope for recovery.

All addicts must undergo recovery, but those with faith are better equipped in the fight against addiction. They believe that with God, anything is possible. They have spiritual tools that enable them to fully commit to and trust in their recovery journey with hope in their hearts. They know that God has a beautiful plan for them, and they have much to look forward to after recovery. Countless people have found that faith is what truly motivated them to commit to treatment. For example, a former addict spent years in support groups and became known as a chronic "relapser." He knew the treatment was not working for him because his innate needs and desires were not being met. He states, "I've never been happier since I gave my life to Christ. I haven't had the desire to use alcohol or abuse drugs since. I realize now that the problem wasn't that I failed in 'working' hard enough… the problem was much deeper; it was in my soul" (ElectricalTrash404, 2022). This does not mean that treatment doesn't work—you should absolutely pursue treatment. The point being made is that faith fulfills our deepest desires and needs, healing the parts of ourselves that could be preventing us from fully recovering.

A REASON TO BE HOPEFUL

Here is one big reason to be hopeful about recovery—about 75% of all addicts in the United States successfully heal from addiction after recovery (Eddie & Kelly, 2021). Let this statistic sink in. Not only are a majority of people seeking help, but they are also finding treatment that permanently works. It usually takes two to five tries, with the median being two. Although people typically have to try more than once to permanently break the cycle of addiction, it is heartening to see that the number of tries is relatively low. Keep in mind that the longer and more intense the addiction is, the more tries it will take to get clean. This is one of the reasons why addressing the addiction in its early stages is so important. In fact, more people have recovered from addiction than those who are currently battling it. The same study found that 80% of people who beat addiction "accomplished at least one major achievement associated with self-improvement and family engagement since overcoming a substance abuse problem—things like getting a new job, completing a university degree, or volunteering" (Eddie & Kelly, 2021). This proves that you can enjoy a happy and successful life after addiction. Your addiction does not have to define you or dictate the rest of your life. You are not alone!

Countless people just like you are seeking recovery and succeeding.

WHY THE SAINTS?

What do the stories of the saints have to do with addiction? More than you think.

The short answer is that the saints' life stories teach us how we should go about our relationship with addiction. These stories of the saints provide us with positive examples of those who beat their addictions and did not let those habits define their lives. Even saints who struggled heavily with addiction found God's grace and were able to do extraordinary things. Studying the saints' lives gives us a concrete idea of how faith in Jesus can guide us toward recovery. For example, we can look at how Venerable Matt Talbot used both spiritual direction and a recovery program to achieve long-lasting sobriety.

The key to these saints' successes was that they recognized Jesus' mercy. They believed that with His grace and mercy, they could do things they could never do by themselves. Do you seek this kind of encouragement in your own life? It can be so easy to believe that you will never be free from your addiction or that your road to recovery will never end. Read about the saints—you will be surprised at their life stories and how much they had to overcome. You will probably find yourself relating to them on multiple occasions, which is precisely why their stories are valuable. Saints are not perfect beings but people who are capable of making mistakes like the rest of us. It is how they choose to turn to God and live their lives in the midst of addiction and recovery that makes them unique.

After reading this book "*The Saints Who Struggled With Addiction*", you will be more positive and hopeful that you can bounce back and begin to live again.

With that said, let's begin. Now we will move on to the stories of the saints, which perfectly illustrate Jesus' mercy. Chapter 1 covers two holy people who struggled with drug abuse, Saint Mark Ji TianXiang, and Blessed Bartolo Longo.

1

SAINTS WHO STRUGGLED WITH DRUGS

Most likely, you do not associate drugs with saints. Saints sometimes seem like otherworldly, perfect people, but they are just as human and imperfect as the rest of us. In fact, there are countless saints who dealt with addiction. While the Catholic Church does not encourage or condone the use of addictive substances and behaviors, it believes that people can achieve holiness despite their struggles.

Hence in the Church, we have saints who struggled with addiction, and they are an excellent example to all of us, especially those of us who are struggling with addiction. No matter how horrible their backstory was, their faith propelled them to change. Not all of them were able to quit their addiction before death, but they still contributed to their communities in unique ways. Their faith allowed them to push through the shame and difficulty of addiction and recovery because they believed in Jesus' mercy and God's plan for their lives.

As we explore the stories of drug-addicted saints, keep in mind how their faith helped them grapple with addiction. Notice how it gave them something to hold on to, no matter how strong the addiction felt. One saint in this chapter died an opium addict but is now a respected holy martyr. Another was able to end his addiction and is now on track to be canonized for his spiritual and charitable contributions to his community. For both of these men, faith allowed them to find a greater purpose beyond addiction. Read their stories to find out more.

SAINT MARK JI TIANXIANG

Basic Biography:

- Born: 1834, in China
- Died: July 7, 1900, in China
- Beatified: November 24, 1946; Saint Peter's Square, Vatican City, Rome, by Pope Pius XII
- Canonized: October 1, 2000; Saint Peter's Square, Vatican City, Rome, by Pope John Paul II

- Feast day: July 7
- Patronage: Drug addicts

Saint Mark Ji TianXiang was born in 1834 to a well-off and respected family in China. He grew up to be a very successful doctor and often treated the poor for free. At the time, opium was a commonly prescribed painkiller. Thus, St. Mark Ji thought nothing of it when he prescribed opium to himself for a painful stomach disease he had. However, even highly skilled doctors at the time did not understand how addictive opium could be. Addiction, in general, was not understood, and developing a dependency on opium, in particular, was considered highly scandalous. Since St. Mark Ji had enjoyed good renown in his community, his addiction became all the more disgraceful for him and his family. He lost his good reputation as a doctor and became a social pariah.

Knowing his addiction was problematic, St. Mark Ji turned to the sacraments. In particular, he would attend mass regularly and continually confess his opium abuse. After a while, the priest hearing his confessions, denied him absolution, believing that St. Mark Ji kept confessing the same sins because he wasn't sorry for them. Neither the priest nor science at that point in history understood how addiction affects the brain. The priest thought that St. Mark Ji was not willing enough to give up drugs. As a result, the priest asked St. Mark Ji to come back to the sacraments after he had quit opium.

During his lifetime, St. Mark Ji was not able to stop abusing opium. Since he did not obtain absolution, he also could not receive the sacrament of the Eucharist for the last 30 years of his life. However, St. Mark Ji continued to show up for mass. Having to stay behind while everyone else went up for Communion must have been very difficult and probably embarrassing at times. What made St. Mark Ji's faith so special is that he still pursued mass and a robust prayer life even though he "couldn't have the full sacramental experience" (Fraga, 2019). He wanted to get as much spiritual nourishment as possible despite the addiction isolating him from certain sacraments, like the Eucharist.

Wanting to prove his faith, St. Mark Ji prayed for martyrdom. We now know this was not necessary for him to get to heaven because he was already trying to quit drugs and had strong faith. However, St. Mark Ji did have his prayers fulfilled. A movement called the Boxer Rebellion swept through China from 1899 to 1901. This movement was run by nationalists who sought to persecute foreigners and Christians. In 1900, the Boxer rebels arrested St. Mark Ji and several members of his family, putting them on trial and demanding that they give up the Catholic faith. On July 7 of that year, he and his family were executed by beheading. He asked that he be executed last so that none of his family had to die alone. What is amazing about his martyrdom story is that he had probably gone many days without having his opium. Even in the midst of extreme withdrawals, he still had the strength to stay true to his faith and think about the needs of his family. This illustrates how faith gave St. Mark Ji a sense of purpose and identity outside of addiction. Even though he died an addict, he died putting what mattered most to him—faith and family—above his cravings. Despite his history of drug abuse, it was not too late for him to show that he was more than his opium addiction. For this reason, St. Mark Ji is the patron saint of drug addicts of all kinds.

Prayer to God through the Intercession of Saint Mark Ji TianXiang:

Lord God, Saint Mark Ji TianXiang struggled with a drug addiction that made him feel distant from his community and his faith. Despite this, he always showed up for what was most important and never gave up hope in Your mercy. Help me put what matters most first in my life, even in the midst of my cravings. May I have a strong spiritual life regardless of my addiction, like St. Mark Ji did.

St. Mark Ji TianXiang, please pray for me! Amen.

BLESSED BARTOLO LONGO

Basic Biography:

- Born: February 10, 1841, Southern Italy
- Died: October 5, 1926, in Pompeii, Italy
- Beatified: October 26, 1980; Saint Peter's Basilica, Vatican City, Rome, by Pope John Paul II
- Feast day: October 5
- Patronage: Anxiety, depression, individuals with a history of satanism

Blessed Bartolo Longo was born on February 10, 1841, in Italy. He was raised in a financially secure Catholic family. His parents were religious, and he grew up with a solid faith—however, Bl. Bartolo started feeling isolated from his religion at ten years old after his father died. Like many addicts, Bl. Bartolo's road to drugs was most likely initiated by grief.

By the time he went to college, Bl. Bartolo was eager to cut all ties with his Catholic faith. He attended the University of Naples during the 1860s when the Catholic Church and the upcoming nationalist move- ment were going head-to-head. As a result, many

young students were getting involved with anticlericalism, atheism, and the occult (Hunter-Kilmer, 2017).
Throughout his college years, Bl. Bartolo experimented
with all three of these. He openly mocked the Church
and constantly tried to persuade others to leave it as he
had done. In addition, he became heavily involved in
satanism and was ordained a satanic priest. The more
Bl. Bartolo fell away from his faith and into satanism
the more involved he became with drugs. He began to
experience increased anxiety, depression, and paranoia
as he continued to nurse his drug addiction. It all came
to a head one night when he had a mental breakdown.
Bl. Bartolo knew then that he could not continue with
drugs and his current lifestyle. During this episode, he
reported hearing the voice of his deceased father
begging him to return to God (Hunter-Kilmer, 2017).
Hearing his father's request is what prompted Bl.
Bartolo to seek help.

He visited an old friend, Professor Vincenzo Pepe, and
told him everything. Professor Pepe encouraged him to
see a Dominican priest who would help him return to
the faith. After seeing the priest for a month, Bl. Bartolo
disowned the occult, atheism, and anticlericalism. He
tried to make amends for his past actions by inviting
people back to the faith and publicly announcing his
change of heart. He was ridiculed by many of his peers
and former associates, especially since he was going

against the popular opinion held by many young people at the time. After six years of this, Bl. Bartolo was ready to face his fears. He walked into a seance for the last time with a rosary in his hand and announced that the occult and other forms of spiritualism were false. At this point, he was free from both satanism and drugs.

Even after his complete conversion, Bl. Bartolo dealt with the shame of his past. At times, he wondered if God truly forgave him and whether he was really released from his past. Once he became so discouraged thinking about it, he lost hope and almost committed suicide. He was prevented from following through when he remembered the advice of the Dominican priest, who told him that teaching others about the rosary could help him get to heaven. He also recalled the comfort of praying the rosary with his family as a child. Inspired by these memories, he found his new purpose and moved to Pompeii. There, he started rosary groups and taught others about Mary. He was instrumental in teaching the locals about Catholic theology and built a basilica for the townspeople. In addition, he took care of Pompeii's poor and orphaned for more than 50 years.

Bl. Bartolo was beatified in 1980 by Pope John Paul II, who called him "a man of Mary " (Hunter-Kilmer, 2017). This is a far cry from his former life as a drug addict and satanic priest, which is what makes Bl. Bartolo's story so extraordinary. Allowing God to forgive him instead of acting on his suicidal thoughts gave Bl. Bartolo an opportunity to do great things in his life. By accepting the mercy of God, he was able to move forward and found a community based on faith and charity. It shows that it is never too late to choose holiness and receive God's mercy, no matter what your past looks like.

What was especially courageous about Bl. Bartolo's conversion is that he was willing to admit his mistakes. His public announcements meant that he acknowledged he was wrong for leading people away from the faith and toward the occult. In addiction, it is often hard to admit your actions to a therapist, let alone to your friends. It is even harder to accept that you have made mistakes when your friends encourage your addiction. There is always a fear that they will leave you or treat you differently. Take heart knowing that Bl. Bartolo was able to make a new life for himself despite the criticism of his old friends. In fact, he found an even bigger and more supportive network of people in Pompeii than he had experienced before.

Prayer to God through the Intercession of Blessed Bartolo Longo:

Lord God, you saw how Blessed Bartolo Longo struggled with shame due to the mistakes of his past even though You had already forgiven him. I know what that feels like, and I ask that you give me the grace to forgive myself for my past actions so that I may fully accept Your mercy. Lord, please teach me that it is never too late to leave my old life behind.

Blessed Bartolo Longo, please pray for me! Amen.

LESSONS FROM THE SAINTS

Here is a summary of the key lessons we can learn from the lives of St. Mark Ji TianXiang and Blessed Bartolo Longo:

- Keep showing up for Mass and for other good activities, even when it's hard.
- Embrace and trust in God's forgiveness so that you can leave your old life of drug abuse behind and move on to a new life – a life with no drug abuse.
- It is never too late to choose holiness or do the right thing. Both saints—one who was still addicted and one who beat his addiction—

were able to choose God throughout their lives.

SUMMARY

Here are the essential points to remember from *Chapter 1: The Saints Who Struggled With Drugs*:

- St. Mark Ji TianXiang died an opium addict but is now known for his dedication to his faith and his courageous martyrdom.
- St. Mark Ji's story teaches us to keep showing up for the good activities.
- Bl. Bartolo Longo was a former satanic priest who dealt with drug use and mental issues, but he is now recognized for building a religious and charitable community in Pompeii.
- Bl. Bartolo Longo's story teaches us to forgive ourselves for what we did in the past because it is never too late to start a new life.

The next chapter will cover the Catholic figures who struggled with alcoholism: St. Augustine Yi Kwang-hon, Venerable Matt Talbot, and Saint Bruno Sserunk-uuma. Through their stories, you will see how their dedication to their faith helped them navigate and overcome alcohol addiction.

2

SAINTS WHO STRUGGLED WITH ALCOHOLISM

Throughout history, alcoholism has been present in society. Unlike more modern addictions, such as technology or shopping, alcohol addiction is nothing new. Thus, we have saints from the earliest times of the Church who experienced the difficulties of abusing alcohol. This chapter will span from the 1700s to the 1920s, demonstrating how widespread this addiction can be.

Each of the saints covered in this chapter recovered from alcohol differently. One saint was given the grace never to desire alcohol again, while another went through an intensive withdrawal program. A third was able to resist relapsing but had instances of temptation. This goes to show that while not all recoveries look the same, all recoveries are worth celebrating. As you read these stories, pay attention to how each saint found freedom from alcoholism and ask yourself how you can apply these techniques to your own life. Taking inspiration from the saints' stories of success can motivate you as you start—or continue—your own recovery.

SAINT AUGUSTINE YI KWANG-HON

Basic Biography:

- Born: 1787; South Korea
- Died: May 24, 1839, in Seoul, South Korea
- Beatified: July 5th, 1925 by Pope Pius XI
- Canonized: May 6, 1984; Seoul, South Korea by Pope John Paul II
- Feast day: May 24

Saint Augustine Yi Kwang-hon was born in 1787 in South Korea; he was born into an aristocratic pagan family. He was allowed to do as he liked and became addicted to alcohol as a young man. After hearing the Gospel, he decided to change his indulgent lifestyle and habits, including excess drinking. At the time, the Catholic faith was spreading in Korea, but it was not accepted by the government. The ruling Joseon Dynasty had made Confucianism the state religion and required all to practice it by law. Thus, St. Augustine took a huge risk by getting baptized, especially since the rest of his family was pagan.

St. Augustine's recovery was unique because he did not feel any desire to drink again after his conversion. He completely turned his life around, sharing the faith with others and opening up his home to other persecuted Christians. While all the saints in this book did have to battle temptation, St. Augustine is the only one who did not have cravings or withdrawal symptoms.

Eventually, St. Augustine and about 100 Korean Catholics were ultimately arrested and beheaded by the government. St. Augustine and the other 100 martyrs were beatified and canonized together as the Korean Martyrs. Group beatification and canonization is a fairly common practice for large groups of people who were martyred together in one place.

You may read St. Augustine's story and assume it doesn't apply to you because he was never tempted to return to drinking. However, there is still a purpose to his recovery story—it can help you envision what life would be like without desiring alcohol. While it is important to acknowledge the struggles of recovery, it is just as important to look to the future with hope. Having a clear idea of what you are working toward—a life that is not controlled by alcohol—reminds you of what recovery is all about. It may take a while to get there, but eventually, your cravings will become weaker and rarer.

In addition, St. Augustine's story can remind you of how fulfilling a life without alcohol can be. Think about the positive changes that happened in St. Augustine's life. He went out of his way to teach others about the faith and was charitable enough to open up his home to others. He even selflessly risked his own safety by sheltering Christians. It is easy to see that he lived a passionate and caring life. When you doubt whether you will be truly happy without alcohol in your life, think about the satisfaction and purpose that St. Augustine found.

Prayer to God through the Intercession of Saint Augustine Yi Kwang-hon:

Jesus, you blessed St. Augustine not to desire alcohol again. While I recognize that I will probably experience withdrawals, help me to remember my ultimate goal, which is a life without alcohol addiction. When I have doubts and temptations, please remind me of how wonderful a life without alcohol can be.

Saint Augustine Yi Kwang-hon, please pray for me! Amen.

VENERABLE MATT TALBOT

Basic Biography:

- Born: May 2, 1856; Dublin, Ireland
- Died: June 7, 1925, in Dublin, Ireland
- Patronage: Alcoholics and Addictions

Venerable Matt Talbot was born on May 2, 1856; he was born into a poor family in the tenements of Dublin, Ireland. Alcoholism was a major problem in his family since his father and all of his older brothers, except the eldest, had serious drinking problems. Thus, Matt was exposed to alcohol abuse from the time he was born. Since his father could not hold a job for long and spent most of the money on drinking, Matt's family had to move often. They moved so much that Matt only attended school between the ages of 11–12 and, there-fore, could not read or write. In an effort to support his family, Matt got his first job at the age of 12 at a beer bottling company. He tried beer for the first time on the job and quickly developed a habit of drinking. By the time he was 16, Matt was a full alcoholic, though some say he was as young as 13. He began to spend most of his time at the bar with his brothers and their friends. It was especially easy for him to develop an addiction because he worked in a beer bottling company and was constantly surrounded by beer. Considering his early exposure, his family history, and those with whom he spent his time, it is easy to see how Matt developed a dependency on alcohol.

His alcohol addiction became so severe that he could no longer hold a job consistently, despite trying to stay employed. Still seeking money to buy alcohol, Matt got into serious debt and began to steal money. In one instance, Matt and his brothers stole a fiddle from a blind street musician so they could sell it. He continued this way of life for about 12 years until he was 28. Looking for a drink but having no money, he stood outside a pub he frequented, hoping one of his friends would offer him a drink. However, each of his friends passed him by on their way in. Matt felt betrayed by the people who were supposed to be his friends, especially since he had spent so much time with them over the years. He was so disgusted that he went home and told his mother that he was taking the pledge to give up alcohol. He went to confession at the Dublin Seminary, and the priest there helped him abstain for three months, then six months. In addition to the priest's support, Matt attended an intensive recovery program that focused on the Eucharist, Mass, Mary, and reading Spiritual books. He learned to read so that he could participate fully in the program, which helped him stay sober for the remaining 40 years of his life. He prac-

ticed a simple lifestyle, constantly giving to the poor, the Church, and charity.

Matt's recovery is a perfect example of how faith and treatment can work hand-in-hand for lasting freedom from addiction. This is so effective because it fulfills both the spiritual and physical needs of the addict. Matt's recovery program gave him a daily schedule, which kept him busy and helped him establish a new lifestyle pattern. He also had access to support through the program and the priest, who became his personal spiritual director. Matt himself believed that faith was the key to quitting alcohol addiction. He had an innate understanding of how difficult it was and that no one could do it alone. However, he knew there was no reason to despair because Jesus could easily break the cycle of addiction. Matt is quoted as saying, "Never be too hard on the man who cannot give up drink. Giving up drink is as hard as it is to raise the dead to life again. But both are possible and even easy for our Lord. We have only to depend on him" (Costa, 2016). This quote is a beautiful expression of trust in God and an encouragement for those who feel like recovery is an impossible feat. Think about how all the odds were against Matt, such as his family history and early exposure. He probably had a genetic predisposition as well. Despite all this, Matt trusted that God would support him in recovery. You must have that kind of trust in God, yourself, and the recovery process. When things do not immediately change for the better and doubts set in, look to Matt's story for proof that anyone can achieve sobriety, no matter the odds.

Another critical lesson we can learn from Matt's story is the importance of making amends. This is certainly a daunting task, for it requires you to acknowledge what you have done and apologize to others who may still be hurting. It may even need you to go out of your way to find people you have hurt, just like Matt did. He repaid every one of his debts exactly and recompensed people for everything he had stolen. He even tried to find the blind fiddler to apologize and make amends. When he could not find him, he gave the money he was going to give the fiddler to the Church and asked for mass to be said for the fiddler. Probably the most important person Matt had to make amends with was his own mother. Even though they were technically never estranged, Matt caused his mother a great deal of pain and contributed to his family's poverty. To make up for this, Matt took care of his mother and let her live with him. It was very painful for Matt to confront his past actions, but it allowed him to truly move on from his past life. You cannot fully embrace recovery if guilt or shame from the past is haunting you, which is why it is worth pushing through the discomfort of making amends.

Prayer for the Intercession of Venerable Matt Talbot:

Lord, you give us the example of Venerable Matt Talbot as a man who seemed completely lost and beyond your grace. In a single moment, you pierced his heart and changed his mind, leading him back to you. Jesus, I pray for this same conversion and transformation in my life for your greater glory.

Venerable Matt Talbot, please pray for me! Amen.

SAINT BRUNO SSERUNKUUMA

Basic Biography:

- Born in 1856; Uganda, Africa
- Died June 3, 1886; Uganda, Africa
- Beatified: 1920; Rome, Italy, by Pope Benedict XV
- Canonized: October 18, 1964; Rome, Italy, by Pope Paul VI
- Feast day: June 3
- Patronage: Excessive drinking, Lust, Improper marriage outside the Church

Saint Bruno Sserunkuuma was born in 1856 in Uganda; he was the son of a Buganda Kingdom chief and was allowed to do what he liked. He grew up with a strong temper and could be violent and aggressive toward others. By the time he was a young man, St. Bruno had an established alcohol addiction, which just added to his other problems. Nevertheless, he had the desire to change and often worked on controlling his vices. When he requested Baptism, people understood that he had the desire to do better and was genuinely trying to change his life. While alcoholism is not just a matter of desire or willpower, his determination to do better did help St. Bruno receive Baptism and defeat his addictive habits.

Inspired by his faith, St. Bruno made several lifestyle changes. For one, he only had one wife instead of having multiple wives and companions. He also practiced charity, giving away all his possessions and property. This was quite a generous gesture for someone of such a high status. He continued to work in the palace as before, but he lived much more simply and always thought of others before himself.

With time, St. Bruno was able to quit drinking. Still, this did not mean that temptations never arose. One notable temptation came at a time of great pain in St. Bruno's life. The ruler of the Buganda Kingdom ordered that all Christians should be arrested and killed. Although he was initially not rounded up with the others, St. Bruno joined his fellow Christians to show his support and to acknowledge his faith publicly. The group of about 45 Christians was forced to take a long and exhausting walk to their execution spot. At one point during the procession, St. Bruno encountered his brother and asked him to bring wine. When his brother came out with the wine, St. Bruno paused and struggled with whether to accept it. He was able to find the strength to refuse, even though he was exhausted and in physical and emotional pain. St. Bruno was later tied to reeds and burned for his faith, along with the others.

In such a time of duress, it was easy to see why St. Bruno almost returned to his old habits and asked his brother for wine. Even though he had a moment of weakness by asking for a drink, he was still able to make a better choice and say no. This moment is relatable for anyone who has struggled with alcohol. It is easy to tell yourself that you can drink one more time or that you will stop drinking once a difficult period in your life passes. Just like St. Bruno, have the courage to ultimately make the right decision and say "no."

Prayer to God through the Intercession of Saint Bruno Sserunkuuma:

Jesus, you inspired Saint Bruno to give up drinking after he heard the Gospel. May I also be motivated by Your Word to change my life. I also ask that You give me strength in tempting situations, just like you gave St. Bruno the power to resist wine in the midst of pain and persecution. Help me believe in myself and in Your grace, which will guide me through every temptation.

Saint Bruno Sserunkuuma, please pray for me! Amen.

LESSONS FROM THE SAINTS

Here is what we can take away from the lives of Saint Augustine Yi Kwang-hon, Venerable Matt Talbot, and Saint Bruno Sserunkuuma:

- Life without alcohol can be purposeful and fulfilling.
- Even if the odds seem to be against you, recovery is possible.
- Making amends may be painful, but it is worth the mental and emotional freedom it will give you.
- Being in a tempting situation does not guarantee that you will return to your old habits. No matter what the situation is, it is always the right time to choose sobriety.

SUMMARY

In this chapter, we learned about various saints who struggled with alcohol addiction. Here is the summary of the main points that were addressed in this chapter:

- St. Augustine Yi Kwang-hon struggled with alcoholism until his conversion. His story illustrates how life without alcohol can be purposeful and fulfilling.
- Venerable Matt Talbot grew up with several alcoholic family members and became addicted at an early age. He proves that anyone can achieve sobriety and make amends for their actions.
- Saint Bruno Sserunkuuma still struggled with temptations to drink. His refusal of alcohol in the midst of pain and persecution motivates us to stay sober during life's most challenging moments.

The topic of the next chapter may surprise you. It is about saints who struggled with Lust. In Chapter 3, learn more about their lives and how their faith helped them overcome their addiction to sex.

Spread the word—Faith in God is the ultimate weapon in the battle against addiction

At the start of this book, I mentioned that people with faith are more resilient against life's biggest challenges —including addiction recovery. Faith empowers you with the knowledge that as hard as life may be right now, God has a beautiful plan for you.

The vast majority of people get over their addictions, and *you* can be one of them. The 12 saints in this book have faced challenges very similar to those you may be undergoing.

Drugs, lust, and gambling caused great anguish even for the 12 saints whose life stories I share in this book. However, despite their uphill struggle, the saints never lost track of their mission—to share the word of God and let other human beings know that they are never alone.

Christ is always watching out for you, protecting you, and believing in you.

I spoke of how many of the saints in this book sought to instill faith in God in other people. Blessed Bartolo Longo, once a staunch satanist, tried to convert even the darkest "children of Lucifer," to

Christ's way, walking into a seance with a rosary in his hand.

He knew of God's power and mercy from his own experience. He wanted to share that it was never too late to be forgiven.

You, too, can be a beacon of light for others who are on the road to recovery from addiction. By encouraging them to read this book, you can empower them with the discovery that they have so much more in common with the saints than they imagined.

In case you think the saints had it easier because of some kind of "innate goodness," think again. Saint Ignatius once said, "Pray as if everything depended on God" and "work as though everything depended on you." Doing good works requires commitment, sacrifice, and discipline. Someone is good when they back their good words with good deeds.

As kind and spiritual as the saints were, they experienced the same withdrawals, temptations, and rejection you may have undergone when you decided to end the hold drugs had over you. By letting others know this truth, you can help them rid their hearts of guilt and shame, and give them greater hope.

By leaving a review of this book on Amazon, you'll show other people who want to free themselves of

the burden of addiction where they can find the inspiration they are seeking.

Simply by telling them how this book helped you and what they can expect to find inside, you'll motivate them to lean on God's power, which is infinite.

Thank you for your support. You may have better and worse days during your recovery, but through faith, you will always have a reason to keep putting one foot in front of the other until the journey becomes more effortless. You will never be defeated when you have God on your side.

Scan the QR code below to leave a review!

SAINTS WHO STRUGGLED
WITH LUST

Out of all the addictions in the world, sex addiction is probably the one that most people think is the least saintly. Despite this common assumption, this chapter delves into the lives of four saints who dealt with sex addiction. All four of these saints were once lustful individuals who had many sex partners. They lived dramatically different lives than the ones they became known for after their conversion.

Just like modern-day addicts, these saints carried a lot of shame. Sex addiction is arguably one of the most secret addictions because most people hide in embarrassment instead of getting help. There is a reason Alcoholics Anonymous is well known, but Sex and Love Addicts Anonymous is not. While no one is obligated to share their addiction, shame should never get in the way of seeking treatment.

When reading these stories, notice how many of these saints grappled with what they did in their past life, just like you and I. However, also take note of how they allowed the mercy of God to heal them. These saints are prime examples of how mercy and grace can renew our lives.

SAINT MARY OF EGYPT

Basic Biography :

- Born: 344; Egypt
- Died: 421; Trans-Jordan Desert, Palestine
- Feast day: April 1

Patronage: Penitents, Chastity, Lust, Converts, Fever, Skin diseases, and Liberation from demons.

Saint Mary of Egypt is a prominent saint of the early Church. She was born in 344 in Egypt. We do not have a lot of verified information about her early life, but we do have many stories of her struggles with sex addiction throughout her teenage years and twenties, as well as details about her conversion. St. Mary ran away from home at the age of twelve to Alexandria and worked as

a prostitute for seventeen years. She did not sell her sexual services just to make a living, it is said that she often did not accept payment because she was primarily seeking pleasure and not money. Eventually, she started accepting so little payment that she had to supply her income by begging and spinning flax.

In an attempt to find more sexual partners, she decided to join a pilgrimage going to Jerusalem for the Feast of the Exultation of the Holy Cross. St. Mary was not motivated by any religious sentiment. She figured the large crowd of pilgrims would give her the best chance of sleeping with as many people as possible. When she arrived in Jerusalem, she followed the crowd to a church that housed the relic of the True Cross Of Jesus. However, St. Mary was physically unable to enter. It was like some invisible force was preventing her from going in. Frustrated, she gave up and went to the side of the Church, where she saw a statue of the Blessed Virgin Mary. Her heart was touched, and she realized how much her desire for sex was harming her body and soul. After praying to Mary for help, St. Mary of Egypt was able to enter the Church. There, she kissed the relic of the True Cross and asked the Blessed Virgin Mary to be with her as she tried to reform her life. After St. Mary left the Church, a stranger suddenly gave her three coins. She used the coins to buy three loaves of bread and went to live in the desert as a hermit. St.

Mary believed that the Blessed Virgin was leading her to a simple, ascetic life in the desert that would bring her true peace. Before going to the desert, she received the sacraments of Baptism, Confession, and the Eucharist.

St. Mary lived alone in the desert for 47 years until a priest by the name of Father Zosimas (or Zosima) ran into her. He often went into the desert during Lent for prayer and fasting. Zosimas was surprised to encounter a ragged old woman in the middle of the desert, but he felt there was something special about her. Women living alone in the desert were quite rare overall, so he may have felt called to figure out why she was there. St. Mary initially tried to run away because she wore little clothing and had not seen anyone else for such a long time. However, Zosimas gave her his cloak and begged her to tell him her story. After she narrated her past life of lust, her conversion story, and her current ascetic lifestyle, he believed she was indeed a special and holy woman. At her request, he met her the following Thursday to give her Holy Communion and agreed to meet her in the same place a year later. When he came back the following year, he found her incorrupt body with a grave marker noting that she had died shortly after he gave her the Eucharist. Moved by her life and miraculous death, he shared St. Mary's story with the other priests in his monastery. From there, the story spread, and St. Mary was widely recognized as a saint.

It is heartening to know that someone who struggled so intensively with sex addiction could turn her life around. It is equally encouraging to see that a recovery story like St. Mary's has been celebrated for such a long time. When you are in recovery, think about how your story could affect your family and community. Even if you do not become as famous as St. Mary of Egypt, you are still leaving a positive legacy for yourself and your loved ones.

Prayer to God through the Intercession of Saint Mary of Egypt:

Lord God, just like Saint Mary of Egypt, I struggle with sex addiction. Despite her struggles, You reformed her life and gave her peace. I ask that You may guide me and strengthen me in my recovery journey so that I may experience that same peace and freedom.

Saint Mary of Egypt, please pray for me! Amen

SAINT VLADIMIR

Basic Biography:

- Born: 958; Russia
- Died: 1015; Ukraine
- Beatified: Unknown
- Canonized: Mid-13th century; unknown Pope (most likely Pope Alexander IV)
- Feast day: July 15
- Patronage: Russia and Ukraine

Saint Vladimir's life before conversion is among the most shocking saint stories, especially for modern readers. Born in 958 in modern-day Russia, St. Vladimir was the illegitimate son of the Grand Prince. His father was an extremely powerful conqueror and had two sons who were in line to take the throne before St. Vladimir. However, St. Vladimir was just as hungry for power as his father and brothers were. He usurped the throne after his father's death by killing his two brothers. When one of his deceased brother's wives refused his advances, he raped her and forced her to become his concubine. Throughout his adult life, it is said that he had 800 concubines and several wives. It is easy to see how St. Vladimir's lust controlled him and made him violent, selfish, and destructive. At the time,

St. Vladimir was a dedicated pagan. He was known to build temples for the pagan gods throughout his empire. In one instance, he sacrificed a father and a son during the dedication of one of his temples.

Surprisingly, it was St. Vladimir's desire for another wife—his eighth—that would introduce him to Christianity. Because of helping the emperor of Constantinople defeat a rebellion, St. Vladimir demanded the emperor's sister as a reward. The emperor refused unless St. Vladimir got baptized and converted to Christianity. Baptism and learning to respect the moral code of Christianity changed St. Vladimir into a completely different person. He had only one wife and no longer kept concubines. He destroyed the pagan temples he built and replaced them with Catholic churches to encourage people to convert to Christianity. St. Vladimir was also known for building schools and libraries throughout his empire. He is now a prominent figure in Russian and Ukrainian history and folklore, as well as the patron saint of both countries.

Out of all the saint background stories in this book, St. Vladimir's might be the most extreme. Both his violence and his lust may initially cause some to accuse him of not being worthy of sainthood. While the serious moral depravity of his old life should not be minimized, it is worth noting the point of his story—

his dramatic conversion and change of heart. While not much is known about exactly why St. Vladimir converted, there are several stories about how it transformed his disposition and lifestyle. In particular, the change in how he treated women was the most drastic. In short, if there is hope for St. Vladimir, there is hope for anyone.

Prayer to God through the Intercession of Saint Vladimir:

Lord God, you have given us Saint Vladimir as an example of how Your grace can change anyone's life for the better. I believe that You can set anyone free from their sex addiction, including me. Regardless of how many mistakes I have made in my past, please help me make things right and start anew.

Saint Vladimir, please pray for me! Amen

SAINT AUGUSTINE OF HIPPO

Basic Biography:

- Born: 354; North Africa
- Died: 430; Hippo, North Africa
- Feast day: August 28
- Patronage: Theologians, Brewers, Printers, Sore eyes

Saint Augustine of Hippo was born in 354 in North Africa to a pagan father and Christian mother but tended to follow his father's beliefs and philosophies. By the time he was sixteen years old, he had completely surrendered to his lust, not thinking about whether what he was doing was right or wrong. His father, who seemed to be having extramarital affairs of his own, found St. Augustine's sexual exploits generally amusing and liked the idea of grandchildren. His mother, St. Monica, was mortified. Despite disagreeing with her son's actions on moral grounds, she did not think a rushed marriage would solve his problems or help his career. Instead, St. Monica continually asked her son to change his ways and, at the very least, not to sleep with married women. St. Augustine eventually settled down with a mistress with whom he had a child, although it is not clear whether he had other sexual partners at this time. After many years of living together, he sent his mistress away to secure himself a high-ranking marriage. According to the marriage contract, he had to be celibate for two years before marriage. St. Augustine could not follow through and took another mistress soon after sending his original partner away.

This whole time, St. Monica was praying for him to convert to Christianity. Her prayers were eventually answered when St. Augustine converted to Christianity. St. Augustine understood that committing to chastity was going to be hard for him even after accepting the Christian faith. He knew that he could only be chaste if he gave up sex altogether, so he remained celibate for the rest of his life. While this may seem extreme at first, this approach is mirrored in many treatment programs. Those in sex addiction programs are not required to give up sex forever, but abstaining from sex for certain periods of time is used to break the cycle of addiction. It serves as a break from giving in to the addiction and gives people time to work through withdrawals. However, rehab patients are required to entirely give up destructive sexual habits, such as having multiple partners, immediately seeking sex in a relationship, and viewing pornography. In this way, those who recover are following St. Augustine's lead.

Due to St. Augustine's robust sexual history, he had a lot to say on the subject. He believed that lust was the product of humankind's rejection of God. He stressed the importance of procreative sex, self-discipline, and chastity before marriage. His writings on the true nature and role of sex have influenced the Church's teachings on sexual morality, even in modern times.

St. Augustine had an acute understanding of sex addiction and the cycle of addiction in general. This quote summarizes it perfectly, "From a perverted act of will a desire had grown, and when desire is given satisfaction, habit is forged; and when habit passes unresisted, a compulsive urge sets in" (James, 1987). What is so interesting about this quote is St. Augustine's choice of the word "compulsive." This word is used time and time again in many standard definitions of addiction. Compulsion is when you are unable to control your actions. It is amazing that a man writing in the fourth and fifth centuries would be able to articulate addiction so well.

Another incredible attribute of St. Augustine's writings is his honesty. In fact, his biographical work the *"Confessions"* reads like a modern-day memoir in the sense that it holds nothing back. One such instance of frankness comes right after his conversion. St. Augustine writes that he asked God, "Give me chastity...but not yet" (James, 1987). He was not afraid, to be honest with both himself and God because he knew he couldn't do it alone. St. Augustine taught that anyone could be saved by God's grace because God's grace heals people's free will. Even though God can never control or take away free will, He can guide us toward what is right. The personal nature of St. Augustine's writings and his teachings about the power of God's grace touched many people, and he became one of the most influential theologians in the history of Western Christianity.

Prayer to God through the Intercession of Saint Augustine of Hippo:

Lord Jesus, Saint Augustine, lived many years with sex addiction, believing that he could not be happy without sex. I know what it is like to feel this way, and I ask that you give me Your grace to change my life, just as You did for St. Augustine. Teach me the true meaning and value of sexuality so that I may align my will with Yours. I believe in the power of Your grace to free me from my addiction, and I thank You in advance for healing me.

Saint Augustine of Hippo, please pray for me! Amen.

SAINT PELAGIA THE PENITENT

Basic Biography:

- Born: 4th or 5th century, Turkey
- Died: 4th or 5th century, Jerusalem
- Feast day: October 8
- Patronage: Actresses

Like St. Mary of Egypt, Saint Pelagia the Penitent is a saint of the early Church. She was born in Turkey in the 4th or 5th century. Not much information is known about her upbringing or her death. We do know that she worked as an actress, dancer, and prostitute. St. Pelagia, who had changed her name to Margarita, was famous for being lustful and materialistic. She publicly appeared around town in famously expensive and immodest clothing to impress people passing by. On one such trip, she passed a group of bishops. All of the bishops were shocked except one called Nonnus, who concluded that they should take as good care of their souls as she did of her outward appearance. Later that day, Nonnus prayed for her conversion and a change in her lifestyle.

Bishop Nonnus' prayers were heard, for St. Pelagia made a rare visit to Church the next morning. Nonnus was preaching about the last judgment and its consequences on salvation. Pelagia was moved by his preaching and asked to be Baptized so she could start anew. However, her conversion was not without struggles. Shortly after her conversion, the devil appeared to her at night and tried to lure her back into her old ways. Even though she was scared, she was able to rebuke him by making the sign of the cross. After a few days of this struggle, the devil never returned.

Another parallel between St. Pelagia and St. Mary of Egypt is that they both decided to live as hermits, which was unusual for women at that time. In St. Pelagia's case, she disguised herself in a monk's habit and traveled to the Mount of Olives in Jerusalem. There, she lived as a hermetic monk and gained a reputation for holiness under the name Pelagius. The fact that she was a female was only discovered after her death.

One of the most interesting episode of St. Pelagia's life was when the devil tried to tempt her. Notice that she responded by simply making the sign of the cross—no grand gesture or magnificent feats were necessary. From this, we can learn not to be afraid when temptation comes our way. Temptation can easily scare us into thinking that we cannot resist our addictions after all. However, simple acts of faith like St. Pelagia's can get us through these moments of fear. Choose your favorite prayer or Bible verse to turn to when you need comfort.

Prayer to God through the Intercession of Saint Pelagia the Penitent:

Lord God, You helped Saint Pelagia recognize the harmful nature of her worldly and lustful life. Furthermore, You inspired St. Nonnus to pray for her healing and conversion. Please place people in my life who will pray for me and support my recovery. Help me turn to You in times of temptation just like St. Pelagia did.

Saint Pelagia the Penitent, please pray for me! Amen.

LESSONS FROM THE SAINTS

This list compiles the main lessons from the stories of St. Mary of Egypt, St. Vladimir, St. Augustine of Hippo, and Saint Pelagia the Penitent:

- Every recovery from addiction, no matter how bad it was in the past, leaves a positive legacy for you and your loved ones.
- God's grace can heal your free will and help you overcome sex addiction.
- When temptation comes, you do not have to be afraid because even the simplest actions like making the sign of the cross, can help you resist and overcome the temptation.
- All these points touch upon hope for recovery. Take encouragement and inspiration from these saints' lives as you navigate your own recovery.

SUMMARY

In this chapter, we covered several saints who struggled with sex addiction. Read the following list of bullet points to review the essential lessons from Chapter 3:

- St. Mary of Egypt and St. Vladimir teach us that recovery is entirely possible, even for those who struggle with extreme cases of sex addiction.
- St. Augustine encourages us to seek God's grace to overcome addiction.
- St. Pelagia the Penitent shows us that even the simplest acts can help us beat temptation.

The next chapter is about Saint Camillus de Lellis and Saint Philip Howard, two saints who struggled with gambling addictions.

SAINTS WHO STRUGGLED WITH GAMBLING

I n this chapter, we will learn about the lives of Saint Camillus de Lellis and Saint Philip Howard. What is so interesting about these two men is that they came from very different backgrounds. One man grew up with an absent father and dealt with emotional trauma, while another came from a prominent family and personally knew the Queen of England. Despite their vastly different lives, they both ended up addicted to gambling and drowning in debt. This illustrates that gambling addictions, or any addiction in general, can affect people from all backgrounds and economic situations.

SAINT CAMILLUS DE LELLIS

Basic Biography:

- Born: 1550; Naples, Italy
- Died: 1614; Rome, Italy
- Beatified: 1742; Rome, Italy, by Pope Benedict XIV
- Canonized: 1746; Rome, Italy, by Pope Benedict XIV
- Feast day: July 14 (In some places it is observed on July 18)
- Patronage: Gambling, hospitals, nurses, physicians, the sick

Saint Camillus de Lellis was born in 1550 in Naples, Italy. He did not grow up with positive role models, especially when it came to his father. His father was known for being violent and hot-tempered and was rarely home. The emotional neglect that St. Camillus experienced made him just as angry as his father, and he became a mercenary soldier as a teenager. A mercenary soldier does not have any affiliation to a particular country or cause but instead fights for whoever offers the most money. After being introduced to gambling in the army, where it was very popular, he soon became addicted. For a time, St. Camillus was able to afford his addiction because he was getting a steady income from his mercenary job. However, he received a wound on his leg, which rendered him unable to fight. He lost his job as a mercenary but could not stop gambling, which left him with no money. With a bad reputation and no funds, St. Camillus had a difficult time finding a job. Even though he was not religious, he finally got employed at a Franciscan friary. A Capuchin monk there who saw his potential inspired him to convert to the Catholic faith. St. Camillus dealt with many gambling relapses, but each time, he would atone for his mistakes and try again. With the help of his spiritual director, St. Philip Neri, St. Camillus was eventually able to beat his gambling addiction.

St. Camillus originally wanted to join the order of Capuchin monks, but his request was rejected because of his chronic leg injury. Instead, St. Camillus traveled to Rome and volunteered at a hospital where he used to be a patient. He noticed that the patients were not receiving adequate care physically, emotionally, or spiritually. This inspired him to form a religious order called Ministers of the Infirm, also called the Camillians, dedicated to giving exceptional care to the sick. St. Camillus believed that if healthcare were motivated by love for God and others, patients would be cared for much better than they were currently being treated. The Camillians had a special branch that provided medical care to soldiers on and off the battlefield. Priests from this branch would wear large red crosses, a symbol that is now synonymous with healthcare and organizations like the Red Cross. Through faith and service, St. Camillus was able to turn his life around.

We can learn a lot about how emotional and familial trauma can cause addiction by studying St. Camillus' life. First of all, his father was uncaring and absent most of the time, which means that St. Camillus had to wrestle with parental neglect. St. Camillus dealt with this trauma by becoming violent and angry and by turning to gambling as a coping mechanism. Gambling was something that could help him forget about his past traumas, and perhaps it gave him a sense of control over his life. However, the opposite was true because gambling eventually caused him to become penniless after losing his mercenary job.

If gambling caused him more problems than it solved, then why did he keep doing it? It all goes back to addiction as a coping mechanism. St. Camillus' circumstances changed, but his trauma was still there. Therefore, he was unable to stop his addictive habits even when faced with negative repercussions. While St. Camillus did not have access to modern therapy, he did have something resembling a counselor, which was his spiritual director. Much like modern therapists, St.

Camillus' spiritual director helped him recognize the harmful nature of his addiction and encouraged him to replace bad habits with better ones. Thus, St. Camillus was eventually able to defeat his gambling addiction through a rich spiritual life and volunteer work. Notice how both prayer and charity provide a distraction from cravings and a new sense of purpose, just like modern treatment strategies do. In this way, St. Camillus is an early model for how to address emotional trauma through counseling and gratifying activities like prayer and volunteer work.

Prayer to God through the Intercession of Saint Camillus de Lellis:

Lord God, You understand how much Saint Camillus struggled with gambling because of emotional neglect. Even though he struggled with relapses, You inspired him to continually seek recovery. Please give me the same commitment to recovery, no matter how many tries it takes. May I find treatments that fulfill me both physically and spiritually, just like St. Camillus. I give my recovery journey to You, Lord, and trust that You will guide me to lasting healing.

Saint Camillus de Lellis, please pray for me! Amen.

SAINT PHILIP HOWARD

Basic Biography:

- Born: 1557; London, England
- Died: 1595; Tower of London, London, England
- Beatified: 1929; Rome, Italy, by Pope Pius XI
- Canonized: 1970; Rome, Italy, by Pope Paul VI
- Feast day: October 25 (or October 19)
- Patronage: Difficult marriages, separated couples, people who are betrayed or falsely accused.

Saint Philip Howard, Earl of Arundel, lived a vastly different life compared to many saints. He was born in 1557 into English nobility and lived a comfortable life in the court of Queen Elizabeth I. In fact, he was one of the queen's favorites. Due to his high station, St. Philip was extremely wealthy, but he was not a good steward of his wealth or title. He lived an extremely worldly life and was so addicted to gambling that he gambled all his money away. This left St. Philip in serious debt, which was very surprising for a man of his station and economic class. St. Philip could not stop gambling and began to sell his wife's belongings so that he would have money to gamble.

Although St. Philip was by no means religious, he decided to attend a debate between two priests, St. Edmund Campion and St. Ralph Sherwin, and several Anglican Protestant ministers and theologians. The two priests were kept under custody in the Tower of London because it was against the Queen's law to practice or spread the Catholic faith. St. Philip was impressed by the priests, who were able to argue persuasively even though they did not have materials on hand as the Anglican theologians did. He was especially moved by St. Edmund Campion, who participated in the debate despite having been tortured on the rack. After seeing this discussion, St. Philip converted to the Catholic faith and changed his lifestyle.

Even though his conversion vastly improved his personal situation, it ultimately put him and his family in danger. If the Queen learned that he had converted to Catholicism, he would be imprisoned. The moment St. Philip sensed that the Queen knew what was going on, he planned to escape secretly with his family. Unfortunately, their ship was stopped, and St. Philip was imprisoned in the Tower of London for his faith and for leaving England without permission. He was sentenced to execution, but the Queen never signed the execution warrant, so he was imprisoned for life. However, St. Philip did not know that the warrant was never signed, so he lived the rest of his life expecting to be executed. While he was imprisoned in the Tower of London, he became friends with another Catholic prisoner, St. Robert Southwell. St. Philip's pet dog would carry letters between their two cells and is featured in the statue of St. Philip at Arundel Cathedral. Both friends found support and encouragement through each other's letters.

St. Philip was imprisoned in the London Tower for the remaining ten years of his life. Although he was allowed books and other reading materials, he was not allowed to see his wife or son, who was born while he was in the Tower. He asked to see them when he was on his deathbed, but the Queen would only grant his wish if he attended an Anglican Protestant church service. He could not accept her conditions, so he died alone without seeing his family. While the end of St. Philip's life was sad, his faith carried him through those ten years in the Tower of London. This is demonstrated by the quote he wrote on his prison wall, "The more affliction we endure for Christ in this world, the more glory we should obtain for Christ in the next" (Bedia, 2020).

Saint Philip's early life is interesting to study for those struggling with a gambling addiction. Notably, it debunks the myth that gambling is permissible if you can afford it. Saint Philip was a wealthy and influential man in the Queen's court, but he was negatively

THE SAINTS WHO STRUGGLED WITH ADDICTION | 63

affected by his gambling problem. It is easy to attribute gambling addiction solely to those who can't afford it, even though gambling affects people from all economic classes. Similarly, it is equally easy to assume that gambling addictions are only problematic if you run out of money. Even though St. Philip eventually did go into debt, he still was addicted to gambling when he had money. While losing a lot of money is a common consequence of gambling, gambling addictions are less about money and more about being unable to stop compulsive behaviors.

Prayer to God through the Intercession of Saint Philip Howard:

Lord God, Saint Philip Howard, displayed courage and commitment to his faith, even when it meant that he was persecuted by his former friends. Give me the strength to pursue treatment and healthy habits regardless of what others say or think of me. Direct my focus toward You and toward the wonderful plan You have in store for my life.

Saint Philip Howard, please pray for me! Amen

LESSONS FROM THE SAINTS

Here is a summary of the key lessons we can learn from the lives of St. Camillus de Lellis and Saint Philip

Howard:

- People often turn to gambling and other addictive behaviors to cope with trauma and other emotional difficulties.
- Prayer and charity are great ways to find purpose during and after recovery.
- Gambling affects all kinds of people from various economic classes and backgrounds.
- A gambling addiction is still a problem, even if you have not run out of money or think you can afford it.

SUMMARY

The following list summarizes the key points from this chapter:

- Much like St. Camillus de Lellis, many people turn to gambling to cope with trauma, emotional difficulties, and mental issues.
- Gambling addiction is a problem no matter how much money you have, as illustrated by St. Philip Howard.
- Faith in God and His merciful grace were instrumental in the recovery of these Saints. With God's help, they could both endure

hardship and enjoy life without the burden of addiction.

END-BOOK REVIEW

Empower others with the most almighty weapon they could ever have—faith.

You now know how much more resilient you can be during addiction recovery when you lean on God.

Simply by leaving your honest opinion of this book on Amazon, you'll show other people that, just like the saints, they can feel closer than ever to God, precisely when they are faced with their biggest obstacles.

LET'S HEAR WHAT YOU THINK!

Thank you for your help. You can help someone else follow the path laid before them by the saints… It's that easy.

Scan the QR code below to leave a review!

CONCLUSION

If there is one lesson to be learned from this book, it is this: There is hope for people with addictions. These stories of the saints are prime examples of how this is demonstrated. Take the saints' lead and turn to Jesus, whose words in Scripture give us the good news that fills us with hope. Hence take some time every day to feed yourself with the Word of God in Scripture; you will be able to discover what God is trying to say to you at that moment. Spend some time with Him and be completely honest about what you are going through.

By reading Scripture, your mindset, thinking patterns, and habits will begin to change and align with God's.

Commit yourself to become better and apply Jesus' words to your life. With an open heart, you will be amazed at what you and God can accomplish together.

If you enjoyed this book, please leave a review on Amazon. The author wishes you the best of luck on your recovery journey.

REFERENCES

Augustine of Hippo. (2023, January 12). Wikipedia. https://en.wikipedia.org/wiki/Augustine_of_Hippo

Bartolo Longo. (2022, October 1). Wikipedia. https://en.wikipedia.org/wiki/Bartolo_Longo

Bedia, S. (2020, September 1). Saint of the month: Saint Philip Howard. St. Ignatius Catholic Parish. http://www.stignatiusmobile.org/saint-of-the-month-st-philip-howard/

BrainyQuote. (n.d.). *Faith quotes.* https://www.brainyquote.com/topics/faith-quotes

Camenga, D., Villanueva, M., & Holt, S. (2022, May 25). How an addicted brain works. Yale Medicine. https://www.yalemedicine.org/news/how-an-addicted-brain-works

Camillus de Lellis. (2022, November 6). Wikipedia. https://en.wikipedia.org/wiki/Camillus_de_Lellis

Catholic encyclopedia, The. (n.d.). New Advent. https://www.newadvent.org/cathen/

Catholic Online. (n.d.). St. Bruno Seronkuma. Catholic Online. https://www.catholic.org/saints/saint.php?saint_id=1848

Catholic terms and definitions. (n.d.). Saint Boniface Catholic Church. https://stboniface-lunenburg.org/catholic-terms-and-definitions

Ciancanelli, S. (2017, August 30). 6 prayers for recovery from addiction. Guideposts. https://guideposts.org/positive-living/health-and-wellness/addiction-and-recovery/6-prayers-for-recovery-from-addiction/

Columba of Rieti. (2022, October 30). Wikipedia. https://en.wikipedia.org/wiki/Columba_of_Rieti

Costa, A. (2016). Combating alcoholism through the example and intercession of Matt Talbot. The Word Among Us. https://wau.org/resources/article/venerable_matt_talbot_patron_saint_of_alcoholics/

Craughwell, T. (2012, June 23). The worst sinners who became saints. Our Sunday Visitor. https://www.oursundayvisitor.com/the-worst-sinners-who-became-saints/

Dumain, T. (2021, January 20). What is drug addiction? WebMD. https://www.webmd.com/mental-health/addiction/drug-abuse-addiction#2

Eddie, D., & Kelly, K. (2021, May 3). People recover from addiction. They also go on to do good things. STAT. https://www.statnews.com/2021/05/03/people-recover-from-addiction-they-also-go-on-to-do-good-things/

Editors of Encyclopaedia Britannica. (2016, March 10). Martyrs of Uganda. Encyclopedia Britannica. https://www.britannica.com/event/Martyrs-of-Uganda

ElectricalTrash404. (2022, February). Comment on the online forum post, Drug addiction: can the Bible help a person cope with drug addiction? Reddit. https://www.reddit.com/r/Bible/comments/t20h42/drug_addiction/

Extra Mile Recovery. (2021, November 12). 7 common challenges people face in addiction recovery. Extra Mile Recovery. https://extramilerecovery.com/blog/7-common-challenges-people-face-in-addiction-recovery/

Fraga, B. (2022, January 25). The life of St. Mark Ji Tianxiang: persevering in faith despite addiction. Our Sunday Visitor. https://www.oursundayvisitor.com/amp/the-life-of-st-mark-ji-tianxiang-persevering-in-faith-despite-addiction/

Galbicsek, C. (2022, September 21). What is alcoholism? Alcohol Rehab Guide. https://www.alcoholrehabguide.org/alcohol/

Glossary of Catholic terms. (n.d.). United States Conference of Catholic Bishops. https://www.usccb.org/offices/public-affairs/catholic-terms

Hall, L. (2020, June 5). 24 bible verses about addiction to help with recovery. Country Living. https://www.countryliving.com/life/inspirational-stories/g32705393/bible-verses-about-addiction/

Harvard Health. (2022, December 6). Understanding addiction. Help Guide. https://www.helpguide.org/harvard/how-addiction-hijacks-the-brain.htm

How to overcome drug addiction: tips for recovery. (2019, November 8). Alvarado Parkway Institute. https://apibhs.com/2017/07/30/how-to-overcome-drug-addiction-tips-for-recovery

Hunter-Kilmer, M. (2017, July 6). He was an opium addict who couldn't receive the sacraments. But he's a martyr and a saint. Aleteia. https://aleteia.org/2017/07/06/he-was-an-opium-addict-who-couldnt-receive-the-sacraments-but-hes-a-martyr-and-a-saint/

Hunter-Kilmer, M. (2017, October 5). Satanic priest turned saint, Bartolo Longo is proof that no one is too lost to be found. Aleteia. https://aleteia.org/2017/10/05/satanic-priest-turned-saint-bartolo-longo-is-proof-that-no-one-is-too-lost-to-be-found/

Hunter-Kilmer, M. (2020, December 26). Saints who struggled with addiction. Aleteia. https://aleteia.org/2020/12/26/saints-who-struggled-with-addiction/

James, F. (1987, July 1). Augustine's sex-life change: from profligate to celibate. Christianity Today. https://www.christianitytoday.com/history/issues/issue-15/augustines-sex-life-change-from-profligate-to-celibate.html

JCRecovery. (2020, September 9). 10 prayers for addiction recovery. JC's Recovery Center. https://www.jcrecoverycenter.com/blog/10-prayers-for-addiction-recovery/

Korean Martyrs. (2023, January 9). Wikipedia. https://en.wikipedia.org/wiki/Korean_Martyrs

Kosloski, P. (2019, July 21). What did Jesus say about forgiveness? Aleteia. https://aleteia.org/2019/07/21/what-did-jesus-say-about-forgiveness/

Lander, L., Howsare, J., Byrne, M. (2013, July 27). The impact of substance abuse disorders on families and children: from theory to practice. National Library of Medicine. https://www.ncbi.nlm.nih.gov/pmc/articles/PMC3725219/

Mann, B. (2022, January 15). There is life after addiction. Most people recover. NPR. https://www.npr.org/2022/01/15/1071282194/addiction-substance-recovery-treatment

Manney, J. (n.d.). *Work as if everything depends on God*. Ignatian Spirituality. Mark Ji Tianxiang. (2022, December 16). Wikipedia. https://en.wikipedia.org/wiki/Mark_Ji_Tianxiang

Mary of Egypt. (2023, January 12). Wikipedia. https://en.wikipedia.org/wiki/Mary_of_Egypt

Matt Talbot. (2023, January 9). Wikipedia. https://en.wikipedia.org/wiki/Matt_Talbot

Mayo Clinic Staff. (2022a, May 18). Alcohol use disorder. Mayo Clinic. https://www.mayoclinic.org/diseases-conditions/alcohol-use-disorder/symptoms-causes/syc-20369243

Mayo Clinic Staff. (2022b, June 18). Compulsive gambling. Mayo Clinic. https://www.mayoclinic.org/diseases-conditions/compulsive-gambling/symptoms-causes/syc-20355178

Mayo Clinic Staff. (2022c, October 4). Drug addiction (substance abuse disorder). Mayo Clinic. https://www.mayoclinic.org/diseases-conditions/drug-addiction/symptoms-causes/syc-20365112

McDonough, B. (2020, October 1). What does the Bible say about addiction? Holdfast Recovery. https://www.holdfastrecovery.com/about/blog/2020/october/what-does-the-bible-say-about-addiction-/

9 tips: how to overcome sex addiction. (2017, January 12). Healing Hearts Counseling Center. http://healingheartscounselingsd.com/9-tips-overcome-sex-addiction/

Nugent, A. (2018, January 24). How an insatiable prince became a patron saint. OZY Live Curiously. https://www.ozy.com/true-and-stories/how-an-insatiable-prince-became-a-patron-saint/83317/

Ouko, J. O. (2014, August 28). From sex addiction to sainthood. Jaluo dot Kom. http://blog.jaluo.com/?p=40570

Pelagia. (2022, April 21). Wikipedia. https://en.wikipedia.org/wiki/Pelagia

Peterson, L. (2017, October 31). St. Mary of Egypt: from a life of sin to sainthood. Aleteia. https://aleteia.org/2017/10/31/st-mary-of-egypt-from-a-life-of-sin-to-sainthood/

Philip Howard, 13th Earl of Arundel. (2023, January 9). Wikipedia. https://en.wikipedia.org/wiki/Philip_Howard,_13th_Ear l_of_Arundel.

Raypole, C. (2022, May 27). Thinking of ditching alcohol? How to make a plan that works for you. Healthline. https://www.healthline. com/health/alcohol/how-to-stop-drinking

Road To Purity, https://www.roadtopurity.com/

Saint Camillus de Lellis. (2020, June 10). My Catholic Life. https:// mycatholic.life/saints/saints-of-the-liturgical-year/july-14-saint-camillus-de-lellis-priest/

Saint Pelagia the Penitent. (2020, August 11). Loyola Press.https:// www.loyolapress.com/catholic-resources/saints/saints-stories-for-all-ages/saint-pelagia-the-penitent/

Segal, J., Smith, M., & Robinson, L. (2022, December 30). Gambling addiction and problem gambling. HelpGuide. https://www. helpguide.org/articles/addictions/gambling-addiction-and-prob lem-gambling.htm

St. Bruno Sserunkuuma. (2020, June 19). Archdiocese of Kampala. https://klarchdiocese.org.ug/about-us/the-uganda-martyrs/st-bruno-sserunkuuma/

St. Bruno Sserunkuuma. (n.d.). Munyonyo Martyrs' Shrine. http:// www.munyonyo-shrine.ug/martyrs/other-uganda-martyrs/st-bruno-sserunkuuma/

St. Mary of Egypt. (n.d.). University of Notre Dame. https://faith.nd. edu/s/1210/faith/interior.aspx?sid=1210&gid=609&pgid=45213& cid=87041&ecid=87041&crid=0&calpgid=61&calcid=53508

St. Pelagia. (n.d.). Catholic News Agency. https://www.catholic newsagency.com/saint/st-pelagia-the-penitent-7

Stagnaro, A. (2016, December 12). Blessed Bartolo Longo, the ex-satanist who was freed through the rosary. National Catholic Register. https://www.ncregister.com/blog/blessed-bartolo-longo-the-ex-satanist-who-was-freed-through-the-rosary

Teaching of Jesus, The. (n.d.). BBC. https://www.bbc.co.uk/bitesize/guides/zkw2vk7/revision/3

Thua, L. (2022, June 29). St. Augustine Yi Kwang-hon - feast day - May 24. Catholic Daily Readings. https://catholicreadings.org/saint-augustine-yi-kwang-hon/

Tyler, M. (2018, May 25). What is addiction? Healthline. https://www.healthline.com/health/addiction

Tyler, M. (2023, January 21). Sex Addiction. Healthline. https://www.healthline.com/health/addiction/sex

Van Sloun, M. (2020, May 12). What did Jesus teach about forgiveness? Archdiocese of Saint Paul & Minneapolis. https://www.archspm.org/faith-and-discipleship/catholic-faith/what-did-jesus-teach-about-forgiveness/

Vladimir the Great. (2023, January 9). Wikipedia. https://en.wikipedia.org/wiki/Vladimir_the_Great

https://www.ignatianspirituality.com/work-as-if-everything-depends-on-god/

Made in the USA
Middletown, DE
25 September 2023

39323521R00046